This book is dedicated to our beloved puppy of seventeen years. Paris, you are everything we want to be and more.

Paris &
The Two Busy Bees

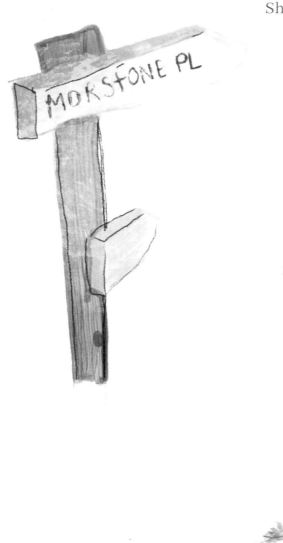

There once was a dog named Paris, who lived in the middle of Morstone Place. Whenever someone was greeted by her, a smile would grow on their face!

She belonged to the Johnsons, who owned, loved and cared for her. She was tiny, sweet and little with fluffy, soft white fur.

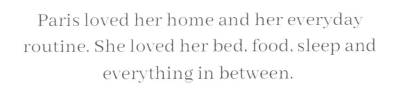

Paris loved her home and her everyday routine. She loved her bed, food, sleep and everything in between.

She would snore and snore and snore and have the sweetest of dreams. Often she would awaken, under the sun's bright, brilliant beams.

Paris would stretch and stretch and stretch, always ready for a brand new day. But she always had to stop, and beg her dad to play.

Zᶻᶻ ᶻᶻᶻ

She started her day with breakfast first, oh how very delicious!

It is so yummy, so tasty, so gooey and it was also super nutritious.

When it was summer, she thought, "What a bummer."
It was always so hot and dry.
She would drink, drink and drink and watch the flowers
wither and die.
Although it was sometimes miserable, the sun's warmth
was simply irresistible.

Although Summer wasn't a really big hit for her, Autumn certainly was. For Paris loved to walk and collect leaves, simply just because....

The weather was perfect, and so was she.
A red jacket she would wear.
All snuggled and bundled, just like a
little Teddy Bear.

When it was Winter, the nights were chilly and cold, but she knew
that she would get a lot more cuddles.
Paris loved being held and smothered in family huddles.

One spring day, like any other. She ate
her brekky and went for a wonder.

Paris sniffed the grass and walked around until she saw her friend. "Good morning, Benny the butterfly". "Aren't you glad Winter has come to an end?"
So Benny replied, "Indeed, it is Paris, now I'll be on my way, too busy to talk, no time to play"!

So Paris continued to trot on her usual way
until she passed by two busy bees having a very
busy day!
They were always moving and going. Paris
always wondered why. Were they going to be
too busy even to say hi? So she asked,
"Hi, what are you guys up to?" The bees said,
"Argh, we are too busy for this, we have far too
much to do!"

After a while, she noticed that some arguing had begun.
"You are so annoying and rude!" bee said to the other. "Well,
you're always winging and whining and annoying. I wished
you'd fly farther".

Paris heard this nonsense and began to ask
with glee, "Please stop fighting! Would you
like to join me for a cup of honey tea?"

o, no no! Be on your way! We have more important things to do

than just sleep and play".

So, Paris left and began to think. "Why are they this way? Can't they see the joy that can be found in every day?"

Although Paris always had a peaceful, sound mind, this little encounter was always on rewind. Paris began to think and pray. "Lord, how can I teach these bees to enjoy their days?"

So she read and studied about their work and the vital work they do when it suddenly came to mind "I know just what to do!"

Paris began to understand why the bees were this way, but there was no chance she would leave them, certainly not astray.

I have a brilliant and wonderful thought! Oh, im so clever.
I'll host a picnic! One where there is tasty food, and i'll pray for springtime weather.

The bees will see how wonderful and a gift life truly is!
They must learn to see it differently before it's all a miss.

So, an invitation was sent out to the whole
backyard and street. I am so excited for all my
friends to meet.

One to Humphrey and Huckleberry, the
retrievers from next door, another to Benny
the butterfly, Rej, her cousin, the busy bees,
and so many more! Finn and Bella were
invited too.
Please bring the fun and your favourite foods
and remember the peanut butter woohoo!

One by one, they all arrived, how wonderful and pleasant, the bees seemed surprised.

There was something different about that day. There was laughter, rest and even time to play.
The time went by in the blink of an eye. With no cake, milk, or peanut butter left in sight, what a joy-filled day with endless delight.

With full bellies and full hearts, the friends began to part.
Off went Benny, Humphry and Huckleberry, saying, " Thank you,
Paris, spring is off to a great start". "Goodbye said Bella, Finn and Rej,
"It sure is getting late".
All the friends left one by one, two by two, said their thank yous, and
marched right out the gate.

After everyone was gone, the two busy bees sat and thought,
" Wow! Now I can see".
"How wonderful it is to be your friend, Paris, when we truly stop
to see that joy does set us free".

The two bees say Paris shows love, joy, peace, patience, kindness
and goodness. They stopped and thought perhaps our life
needed newness.

HOME

The bees sang back to the hive, the flowers were full, and more colours were alive. The bees said, " Our life is sweet and hard to beat. How wonderful and fun our life has become".

It was all thanks to their friend Paris, who showed the busy bees how to simply be.

In a world full of distractions and despair, remember its the little
things we remember in our prayers.

Learn these lessons from Paris, whose life was simple and true. For
when you look inside her heart, this life is open to you!